H̶e̶r̶c̶u̶l̶e̶s̶:
By the Sword

A novel by Timothy Boggs
based on the Universal television
series entitled:
Hercules: The Legendary Journeys™
created by Christian Williams
Executive producers Sam Raimi
and Robert Tapert

Level 2

Retold by John Escott
Series Editors: Andy Hopkins and Jocelyn Potter

Pearson Education Limited
Edinburgh Gate, Harlow,
Essex CM20 2JE, England
and Associated Companies throughout the world.

ISBN 0 582 81705 6

First published by Puffin Books 1997
This edition first published 1999

Typeset by Digial Type, London
Set in 12/14pt Bembo
Printed in Spain by Mateu Cromo, S.A. Pinto (Madrid)

For a complete list of the titles available in the Penguin Readers series
please write to your local Pearson Education office or to: Marketing Department,
Penguin Longman Publishing, 80 Strand, London WC2R 0RL.

Contents

conteúdo

Introduction

Hercules! Half man, half god! Stronger than any man in the world! He fights for the weak and is always ready to help others when they are in danger.

Hephaestus, God of Fire, makes a beautiful but dangerous Sword of Fire for his king, Zeus. But raiders steal the sword and Hercules must get it back before it is used against the men, women and children in towns and villages all over the country. Hercules cannot leave the Sword of Fire in dangerous hands. He must do something – and quickly!

Hercules: The Legendary Journeys is a Studios USA television series, starring Kevin Sorbo as the famous half man, half god, Hercules. People watch each one-hour show in countries all over the world – Australia, Belgium, Brazil, Canada, China, Greece, Hong Kong, Italy, Mexico, South Africa, Ukraine, Venezuela, and many, many more.

Chapter 1 A Night in the Forest

The two men sat near the fire. It was the only light in the forest outside the village of Markan that night.

'I'm not happy about this, Trax,' the first man said.

He was big and tall. Trax was smaller, but as strong as the other man.

'You're never happy about things, Castus,' said Trax. His friend was often unhappy at night. It wasn't important. Living was important. And stealing. Trax was quite good at stealing, but he was not rich from it.

'But I'm *going* to be rich,' he thought, and put his hand on the box between them. 'It took us a week to get this, and four of our men died. Now there's only Castus and me.'

'Is he going to bring the money?' said Castus.

'Yes,' said Trax. 'He – wait, I can hear something!'

A man came through the trees. He was tall, and they saw his sword in the light from the fire.

Trax got the box, and stood up slowly.

'Have you got it?' the man asked him.

Trax was afraid, but he tried not to show it. 'Have you got the money?' he said.

The man threw a small bag to Castus. Trax gave the man the box, and he started to open it.

'Trax,' said Castus.

Trax watched the man open the box. He wanted to get away. Far away, across the sea.

'Trax,' Castus said again.

'What?' said Trax.

'There's no money in the bag, Trax,' said Castus.

The man took something out of the box.

1

'No money?' said Trax.

'No,' said Castus. 'He didn't give us our money.'

Suddenly there was a big red flame in front of the two friends. And they began to cry out . . .

Chapter 2 A New Friend for Nikos

It was a warm afternoon in the village of Markan, and women went to the square in the centre to talk and do their shopping. Some laughed, and noisy children ran in and out of the small streets near the square.

A man sat at one of the small tables inside Nikos Veleralus's small hotel. Nikos watched him eating and smiled. People liked to come to his hotel. His food and drink were good, and there were six rooms for people to sleep in.

Suddenly a small boy from the street ran into the hotel. He

It was a warm afternoon in the village of Markan.

2

Bones = οστά

was about eight or nine years old. Nikos did not like dirty little
street boys. They laughed at his big nose.

'Bones!' cried the boy.

'Sorry,' said Nikos. 'I gave them to the dog last night.'

'No!' said the boy. 'Bones – in the forest!'

'Animals' bones?' asked Nikos.

'No, people's bones,' said the boy. He began to cry. 'Dorry –
Dorry jumped on me and we fell down, and we . . . we fell on –
we fell on . . .' He stopped.

'All right, boy, all right,' said Nikos. He put a hand on the boy's
arm. 'Take it slowly. Tell me when you're ready.'

'I told you!' cried the boy. 'Dorry and me fell on some bones
in the forest. They were people's bones. Dorry was afraid and ran
home, and I did too.'

'Home?' said Nikos. He looked carefully at the boy. 'Bestor, is
that you?'

'Yes,' said his son, and started to cry again.

'I thought you were a dirty street child!' said Nikos.

'Sorry, Father,' said Bestor.

'Go and have a bath! Now!' said Nikos.

Suddenly, there were noises outside. Nikos heard a woman cry
out, and he ran out into the street.

'Oh, no!' he said. 'It's the Corsco brothers.'

When the two Corsco brothers wanted to steal money or
food, they came to the village. They were bigger and stronger
than any man there; sometimes they broke tables in half with one
hand; or ran after the village women.

The brothers were in the square with Lydia Cember and her
younger sister, Dutricia. The Corsco brothers laughed and
pushed the women between them.

'Father, it's Lydia!' cried Bestor, from the door of the hotel.

'Yes,' said Nikos, angrily. He and the boy loved Lydia, and she
loved them.

3

'Nikos!' cried Lydia, and started to run to him. Francus Corsco pulled her back and put his arms round her.

Nikos ran into the hotel and got a big stick from behind the bar, then ran outside again. He saw Francus laughing and pulling Lydia's skirts. Nikos ran across. He tried to hit Francus with the stick, but Francus pulled it out of his hand easily, and said, 'Die, you dog!'

Francus had a hand across Nikos's mouth and was ready to hit him with the big stick. But suddenly a quiet voice said, 'Please stop that. I'm trying to eat.'

Then everything happened very fast. Suddenly, the hand went from Nikos's mouth, and he fell back on to the road. He saw the man from the hotel pull the stick from Francus's hand and throw it away. He saw the man throw Francus away, too, then move across and throw Sinius Corsco away from Dutricia.

The man looked at Nikos. 'Are you OK?' he said, and helped him to get up.

'Yes, thank you,' said Nikos. Lydia ran and threw her arms round him, and began to cry. Then Bestor ran across to him, but looked up at the man.

'Wh– what's your name?' Nikos asked the man.

After a long time the man said, 'Hercules.'

Everybody turned to look at him. Some put hands to their mouths. Others said, 'It's the famous Hercules!'

Before Nikos could speak, Hercules turned to the boy and said, 'Now, tell me about the bones in the forest.'

Chapter 3 Zorin's Raiders

Hercules and Nikos followed Bestor through the trees in the forest. They walked for more than an hour before the boy said, 'There!' and they saw the men's bones.

'Somebody made a cooking fire here,' said Hercules.

'Yes,' said Nikos. 'A month or two ago, do you think? But why didn't anybody find them before this?'

Hercules moved nearer with his sword in his hand. He pushed the bones with the sword, and looked at the grass round them. The grass was black.

'They burned,' said Nikos.

'Yes,' said Hercules. 'But the grass only burned near the bones. These men died before they could move. No small cooking fire did this, it was something much worse.'

'But what?' asked Nikos.

Hercules had no answer.

They walked back to the village some minutes later.

'Perhaps the gods were angry with these men,' said Nikos, 'and killed them with swords of flame.'

Hercules smiled but said nothing. He saw people waiting for them in the village square. And for the first time he saw some trees and old carts, ready for the villagers to push across the road. 'They're afraid,' he thought.

That night, Bestor ran into Hercules' room at the hotel.

'Raiders!' he cried, and ran out again.

Hercules followed him. The trees and carts were across the road into the village now. He saw Nikos talking to about twenty men in the square. Some of them had swords, others had bows and arrows or heavy sticks. He saw some women carrying water, ready to put out any fires, and he saw Lydia taking some children home.

Hercules went across to Nikos. 'Raiders?' he said.

'It's Zorin,' said Nikos. 'His raiders kill and steal, and take the women from the villages. King Arclin's men tried to stop them, but they couldn't. Tonight they're coming to Markan.' He looked at the carts. 'But we're ready for them.'

Hercules went to the carts and looked out into the night.

He saw about ten or twelve raiders coming down the road.

Hercules moved nearer with his sword in his hand.

They carried swords. 'Are there are more behind them in the darkness?' he thought.

The raiders stopped near the carts. A big man with a sword cried, 'You in there! We don't *want* to kill you. Give us food, drink, women . . . and all your money.'

'And the village?' asked Nikos.

'We're going to burn that down,' said the big man. His friends laughed.

Hercules jumped on to one of the carts and looked down at them. 'You kill nobody,' he said. 'You burn nothing.'

The big raider looked at his men, then looked back and smiled. 'And who are you?' he asked.

'A friend,' Hercules said before Nikos could tell them.

'Listen, friend,' said the big raider. 'Go back home. I want to talk to the man with the big nose.'

'*You* go home,' said Hercules.

The raider got angry. 'No more talk!' he said. And with a cry to his men, he started to move near the carts. His men followed him. Arrows flew from men with bows in the houses, but not many of them hit the raiders. The big raider started to climb through the carts. But he was too slow; Hercules pulled him up and threw him across into the square. The other raiders pulled the carts away from the road, and they and the villagers started to fight in the square.

'Watch the road for more raiders!' Hercules called to the men in the houses. Then he jumped down from the cart and started to fight with the others.

It was a hard fight, but everything happened quickly. Men fell to the floor, swords flew from hands and across the square, and there were cries of 'Aaagh!' and 'Help me!'

Then, suddenly, the fighting stopped and Hercules had some time before it started again. The raiders quickly ran to stand together with their swords in their hands. They waited for the villagers to move again.

Then, suddenly, the fighting stopped and Hercules had some time before it started again.

Hercules pulled a small tree from under the carts.

'There are too many of them,' said Nikos.

'Watch,' Hercules said, and moved across to the raiders.

Nikos called 'Follow him!' to the other villagers.

The big raider said something to his men, and they ran to the carts and the road. Hercules threw the tree at them, and they fell down on their backs. He jumped over them – he wanted to get to the big raider.

The raider's sword was above his head, ready. But Hercules put a hand round the raider's foot and pulled him down with the others. Then Nikos and his men jumped on them and took away their swords.

Hercules told Nikos, 'Tie the hands and feet of the big man, and two more of them.'

8

'And the others?' asked Nikos.

'Take their swords from them, and tie their hands together, but not their feet,' said Hercules. 'They're going back to Zorin to tell him everything.' He pulled one of the raiders across to him. 'Say to Zorin, "Hercules is in Markan. Stay away!" OK?'

'OK, OK!' said the raider.

Hercules turned to Nikos. 'Can you leave the hotel for a day or two?' he asked.

'Yes,' said Nikos. 'But why?'

Hercules looked at the three raiders. 'We're going to take the big man and the other two to King Arclin,' he said.

Chapter 4 The Sword of Fire

The fire was warm, but the night was cold. The raiders were in the back of the cart. They slept noisily. The big raider's name was Theo. 'Theo the Killer,' his men called him. Nikos slept near the fire.

Hercules listened to the night. 'What's wrong?' he thought. 'I don't think Zorin is going to come here to get Theo and his friends. And King Arclin is going to be happy to talk to the three. He can make them tell him things about Zorin's plans – or they'll die. And Arclin's going to be happy with the villagers of Markan. So why am I not happy?'

He heard a small noise. 'A night bird?' he thought. He heard the noise again. Then it stopped, and a voice said, 'Hercules, you're a very difficult man to find!'

◆

There were two mountains many kilometres to the east. Far below, between them, were Zorin's tents. Zorin's tent was the biggest. There were lights and a fire inside it, and Zorin sat in a big chair under one of the lights. He looked at the raider in front of him.

'It was one man?' said Zorin. 'What was his name?'

'Her-Hercules,' said the raider, and fell down on the floor.

Zorin looked at the man next to him. 'Is this true, Crisalt?' he asked.

'The other six say the same thing,' said Crisalt.

'And this Hercules took three of my men away, is that right?' said Zorin.

'Yes,' said Crisalt. 'Theo and two others. He's taking them to King Arclin.'

Zorin got up and went to stand over the raider. 'And he said, "Hercules is in Markan. Stay away!" Is that right?'

'Y-yes,' said the raider.

Zorin kicked the man hard, then walked behind his chair to a big box. There was a red light inside the box. 'Crisalt!' he said. Crisalt went and stood next to him. 'Theo calls himself, "Theo the Killer," is that right?' He put a hand on the box.

'Yes,' said Crisalt.

'He made a bad mistake,' said Zorin. 'He must die.'

He moved his fingers slowly along the box – and thought, 'What happens now? The king asks Theo questions. That's OK. And then Theo gives money to the king's men, they look away, and Theo gets out. That's OK, too. Then he comes back here and . . . and I kill him!' He smiled.

He turned to Crisalt. 'We have the Sword of Fire,' he said. 'It's not going to be easy, *but Hercules is going to die.*'

◆

'Go away, Hermes,' Hercules told the thin little man next to him near the fire.

'I can't,' said Hermes. 'I have something to tell you.'

The gods always sent Hermes to tell things to people. 'Go on,' said Hercules. 'I'm tired and hungry, and –'

'OK, but you aren't going to like it,' said Hermes. 'Hephaestus made a beautiful sword for the god Zeus. A sword of fire. It *makes* fire and burns things. But somebody stole the sword from Hephaestus' house, and he wants you to get it back.'

Hercules thought hard. 'Hephaestus is a good brother to me,' he said to Hermes after a minute. 'And I can't leave the sword in dangerous hands. I don't like it, but I must get it back for Zeus. I know that Zeus is my father, but he did nothing to stop Hera killing my wife and children, and I don't speak to him now. But . . . well, OK.'

Hermes smiled, and flew off into the night.

Hercules went to sleep. It was early morning when he opened his eyes again – and saw a man with a sword in his hand.

The man looked down at him. 'Get up!' he said. 'The king wants to see you.'

Hercules put a hand out for his sword and jumped up angrily. 'Say "please", or I –'

'Wait, Hercules!' said Nikos, and ran across. He turned to the man. 'This is the famous Hercules.'

The king's man looked at Hercules – and smiled. 'I'm sorry,' he said. 'I didn't know –'

'It's OK,' said Hercules, after a minute. He smiled back.

There were twelve of the king's men moving round the cart and the raiders.

'What's happening?' Hercules asked Nikos.

'King Arclin sent some of his men to take us to him,' said Nikos.

'So he knows we're coming,' thought Hercules. 'How?' But he said nothing.

They moved very fast all that day, and arrived at the city late in the afternoon. Theo was very quiet.

'He's afraid,' thought Hercules.

Chapter 5 King Arclin and the Big Plan

King Arclin was a young man. He was very small, he wore beautiful clothes and he had short brown hair. He sometimes made mistakes, and people often laughed at him behind his back.

'Are these the raiders?' he asked.

'Yes, sir,' answered Arclin's captain. Theo and the other two raiders were on the floor in front of him. He looked across the room at Hercules and Nikos. 'And this is Hercules, and Nikos of Markan,' he told King Arclin.

'Bring them to me!' said Arclin. He did not look at Hercules or Nikos.

The captain looked at Hercules and said the word, 'Come here!' with his mouth, but made no sound.

Hercules did not move, and he put a hand on Nikos's arm before Nikos could move.

'Come here! Now!' the captain mouthed again.

After another minute, Hercules moved and took Nikos with him. They stopped behind the raiders.

'I'm sorry,' said Hercules. He smiled. 'My friend and I are a little tired.'

Arclin turned and looked at Hercules. 'You're very famous,' he said. 'These raiders were a big problem to me and my people. I thank you.' He put up a hand, and some of his men took the raiders away. Then he took a small bag from his coat and threw it to Hercules. There was money inside it.

Hercules caught it and gave it to Nikos. 'Very nice,' he said.

Arclin smiled with his mouth but not with his eyes. Then he said, 'The people of the little village of Drethic want us to protect them from Zorin and his raiders. Isn't *that* nice? *Another* village for King Arclin.' He gave a little laugh.

Hercules smiled coldly. 'Drethic was not a little village the last time I saw it,' he thought. 'And it wasn't King Arclin's village.

12

How many more are asking for Arclin's men to protect them from Zorin?'

'And now I must go,' said Arclin. 'Thank you again, Hercules and Nikos.' He turned away.

'Sir?' said Nikos, before Hercules could stop him.

Arclin looked back. 'What is it?' he said.

'Sir,' said Nikos, 'the raiders ... perhaps they're going to come back ... There's Zorin's Fire, you see ... we can't ... Hercules has many places ...'

'Tell your people, "Do not be afraid. King Arclin is going to protect us now." All right?' he said, coldly.

'Yes,' said Nikos. 'Yes, thank you, sir. It's very good of you, sir. Thank you.'

'Yes, it is good of me,' said Arclin, and he walked away.

The captain came across to Hercules and Nikos. 'Get out of here before tonight!' he told them quietly. Then he went after the king.

'Is something wrong, Hercules?' asked Nikos.

Hercules thought for a minute, then said, 'Arclin knows something, and he thinks that I know it, too.'

'Do you?' asked Nikos.

'Yes, I think I do,' said Hercules.

'Is it something bad?' asked Nikos.

'Yes, my friend,' said Hercules. 'Arclin's captain was right. We must get away from here before tonight. We don't want to die here.'

The sky was nearly dark when they walked out of the city.

'I don't understand,' said Nikos. 'Why does King Arclin want to kill us?'

'Not you, me,' said Hercules.

'But I'm with you,' said Nikos. 'I can't die. My son ...'

'You're not going to die,' said Hercules. 'Yes, perhaps he wants us dead, but it's not going to happen.'

◆

There were too <u>many</u> dark corners on the road back to Markan.

There were too many dark corners on the road back to Markan. Hercules did not like it. 'How am I going to get Hesphaestus' sword?' he thought. 'Is it "Zorin's Fire"? Yes, that's it! But then, why does Zorin only take small towns and villages? Why not big places ... Athens, or ...?' He stopped suddenly, and Nikos walked into his back.

'*How* does King Arclin stop him?' said Hercules. 'Zorin has the strongest, most dangerous sword in the world – Hephaestus' Sword of Fire! No man can stop that.'

'But *does* King Arclin try to stop him?' said Nikos.

Hercules looked at him. 'No! You're right!' he said. 'Arclin *doesn't* stop Zorin because Zorin and he are working together! They want to get their hands on all the towns and villages – and all the money in those towns and villages. That's their Big Plan!'

Nikos looked past Hercules, and was suddenly afraid.

'What's wrong?' said Hercules. Then he turned and saw Hermes in the sky near them. 'What now, Hermes?' he said.

'Why don't you go and get the sword before Hephaestus gets very angry?' said Hermes.

'Where is it?' said Hercules. 'Do you know?'

'Yes, I came back to tell you,' said Hermes. 'But that's not all.'

'What are you talking about?' said Hercules.

'Brother, you're not going to like this,' said Hermes.

Chapter 6 The Problem of Hercules

'Let's go into the trees,' said Hercules, and he and Nikos followed Hermes off the road.

'Go to sleep,' Hermes said to Nikos.

'No, no,' said Nikos. 'I'm not tired. This is all too exciting.'

'I think you *are* tired,' said Hermes. He moved a hand over Nikos's head – and Nikos went to sleep.

15

pretty = bonito

Hercules looked at Hermes. 'Zorin's Fire is Hephaestus' sword,' he said. 'Right?'

'That's right. Some men stole it from Hephaestus,' said Hermes. 'They gave it to Zorin – or two of them did. The others burned and died. Hephaestus is very angry. You must get it back in four days, Hercules, or he's going to . . . you know.'

'Where is Hephaestus?' asked Hercules.

'Do you know the mountains north of King Arclin's city?' said Hermes.

'He's under one of those?' said Hercules. 'But listen, how can I get the sword and give it back to Hephaestus in four days?'

'That's easy,' said Hermes. 'Zorin and his men have their tents down between those mountains.'

'So why can't Hephaestus come out and get it?' asked Hercules.

'He's not very pretty, remember?' said Hermes. 'Dogs and small children are afraid of him. People laugh at his face and he gets angry about it. We don't want him to get angrier and angrier, and then burn everybody.'

'First I must get Theo and his friends away from King Arclin,' said Hercules.

'How are you going to do that?' said Hermes.

Hercules looked at Hermes and smiled slowly.

'No!' said Hermes. 'No, I can't carry you!'

'Why not?' said Hercules. 'It's not far.'

'No, I . . .!' said Hermes. He looked off into the dark. 'Did you hear that?' And he flew up into the dark night sky and away.

An angry Hercules kicked a tree. 'Hermes isn't going to help me,' he thought, 'so I must do it myself. I can get to King Arclin's city before it gets light. After that I –'

There was a noise, and suddenly Hermes was back. 'I hope you're happy now,' he said, and pushed somebody in front of him.

Hercules smiled. 'Hello, Theo,' he said.

♦

16

Clever = inteligente

King Arclin thought about the famous Hercules. 'He's too clever. And dangerous. He must die before the Big Plan is finished. Zorin has the Sword of Fire now, and things are moving quickly. But I'm as clever as he is. Towns and villages come and ask me to protect them from him. I'm going to agree with Zorin and his plans. I'm getting rich because of him!' And he laughed.

The captain came into the room. 'Sir!' said the captain. 'The three raiders – they're not there!'

'Not there?' said Arclin. 'How did they get out?'

'I – I don't know, sir.'

'Did you send men after them?' said Arclin.

'Y–yes, sir,' said the captain.

'All right,' said Arclin. 'Come back as soon as you know anything new.'

♦

barraca

Zorin walked up and down in his tent. 'I want to know,' he told Crisalt.

'We all want to know,' said Crisalt. 'But we must wait for Theo and his men to get here tomorrow.'

Zorin could hear his men moving round the camp and talking together. Things were too quiet for them. They liked a good fight.

'Hercules and his friend from the hotel are going back to Markan,' said Crisalt. 'Did you know?'

'Hercules is a danger to my plans,' said Zorin. 'I must work with King Arclin –'

'But not for long,' said Crisalt with a smile.

'No, not for long,' said Zorin. 'I don't like it. And now I have the problem of Hercules.'

They were quiet for a minute, then Crisalt said, 'Why doesn't Hephaestus come and get his sword? I don't understand it.'

17

Zorin did not answer, but he thought, 'Because Hephaestus is getting Hercules to do his dirty work for him!'

♦

Nikos opened his eyes and saw Hermes looking down at him. 'Where's Hercules?' he asked.

'He left,' Hermes told him.

'Where did he go?' said Nikos. 'Why didn't he take me with him?'

'He couldn't. Now, I'm taking you home,' said Hermes. 'Are you ready?'

He took Nikos's hand, and suddenly . . .

'We're flying!' cried Nikos.

Chapter 7 A Visitor for Zorin

'You walk too fast,' Theo told Hercules. He was cold and tired. After a minute or two they moved off the road and into the trees. Hercules made a small fire and they sat down.

'When we get to Zorin's tents,' said Hercules, 'say to the men, "I lost the other two in the dark, then Hercules caught me. He wants to see Zorin." OK?'

Theo didn't answer. It was no problem getting away from King Arclin. Give some money to one of Arclin's men; it was easy. But this was different. This *was* a problem.

'They're going to kill me,' he said. 'Zorin never wanted me to be one of his raiders. He only used me to get to you.'

'Perhaps,' said Hercules.

'Do you want me dead?' said Theo, angrily.

'No,' said Hercules. 'I want to get into his tent, and you can get me in. Now, tell me everything about the place – where is Zorin's tent?'

'It's at the back of all the other tents, and it's black,' said Theo.

Hercules asked some more questions, then suddenly they heard people talking on the road. Somebody called, 'We know you're here. Come out!'

Hercules saw four men with swords, and he moved quietly back into the darkness. Theo was too tired to move.

'And I thought Arclin never sent his men after Zorin's raiders,' thought Hercules. 'I was wrong.'

Arclin's men stopped. One of them came through the trees. 'Hello,' he said to Theo. He had his sword in his hand. Another, smaller man moved up next to him.

'Wh–where are my friends?' asked Theo.

The small man laughed and said, 'Did you lose them? Get up – I don't like killing a man on the floor.'

'Good,' said Hercules behind them.

They turned, but were too slow. Hercules threw the first man into the two on the road. Then Hercules hit the other man hard.

Then Hercules hit the other man hard. He moved quickly.

19

He moved quickly to the other three and hit two heads together. The first man was on his feet again now, and tried to kill Hercules with his sword. Something moved in the darkness behind the man. He started to turn and hit something with his sword. Then Theo hit him on the head. Now all four of Arclin's men could not move.

'Can I sit down now?' said Theo, weakly.

'Not here,' said Hercules.

But suddenly Theo fell. 'His sword ... got me ... I ...' And he died.

♦

'Stop!'

Four of Zorin's men stopped Hercules on the road into the camp. Behind them, four more came out of the trees.

'What do you want?' one of them asked.

'I want to see Zorin,' said Hercules. 'My name's Hercules. I think he's looking for me.'

They tied his arms and his legs, and put him in a small, dirty tent. He waited all morning and all afternoon that day, and they gave him no food or water. He could hear men outside. That evening, he had a visitor. The visitor brought him some bread and water.

'You hungry?' said the visitor.

Hercules turned and showed him his tied hands. 'How can I eat?'

'I'm Crisalt,' said the visitor. 'You're Hercules.' He called to a man outside the tent. The man came in and untied Hercules' hands. Then he gave Crisalt a sword and went outside again.

Hercules started to eat and drink. 'When can I see Zorin?' he asked.

'Later,' said Crisalt. 'Why are you here?'

'I think Zorin wants to see me,' said Hercules.

'Do you want to kill him?' asked Crisalt.

'With all his men here?' said Hercules, and smiled.

'Then I don't understand,' said Crisalt.

'It isn't important for *you* to understand,' said Hercules. 'Only Zorin must understand.'

'So you're not going to tell me,' said Crisalt. 'Then you must stay here.'

'A waiting game?' said Hercules.

'Zorin doesn't play games,' said Crisalt. He was angry. He took the sword and went outside.

Hercules waited.

Crisalt came back. His face was red. 'Listen, Hercules,' he said. 'Zorin doesn't play games.'

'You told me that before,' said Hercules.

Crisalt moved nearer with his sword, made an angry noise – and went out again.

Chapter 8   Flames in the Sky

'What happened?' asked King Arclin, and the captain told him.

'All of them?' said Arclin, angrily.

'One of them lived, sir,' said the captain.

'Who did this to your men, do you know?' asked Arclin.

'We know, sir,' said the captain. 'We found one of the three raiders near them. He was dead.'

'But the other two raiders were not with him?' said Arclin.

'No, sir. They're dead.'

'Good.' King Arclin looked at his captain. 'Tomorrow you must find an answer to our ... problem. You must make a plan, and come and tell me.'

The captain was afraid, but he spoke. 'Sir, the men are not ready,' he said.

Arclin did not want to hear this. 'Only half of Zorin's men are at the camp,' he said. 'Are half his men better than all your men, captain?'

'No, sir!' said the captain.

'Then bring me a plan, captain!' he said.

He waited for the captain to go, then tried to think. 'So the Big Plan must happen a month or two sooner,' he thought. 'And after tomorrow night, nothing can stop me! Nothing!'

◆

Crisalt went into Zorin's tent.

'Yes?' said Zorin. 'You have something to tell me?'

'Yes,' said Crisalt.

'About Hercules?' said Zorin.

'Not Hercules,' said Crisalt. 'Something worse.'

'Tell me,' said Zorin.

'Arclin's men killed two of our men, but not Theo,' said Crisalt.

'What!' Zorin said angrily. 'Arclin's men killed them?'

'Yes.'

'But Theo got away?' said Zorin.

'Yes,' said Crisalt. 'We think he got away in the fight.'

Zorin laughed. 'So he's far away by now. OK, good luck to him!'

'What are we going to do about Arclin?' asked Crisalt.

'When all the men are back, we're going to send him a little Fire,' said Zorin. 'But tell me now – what did Hercules say?'

Crisalt told him, then asked, 'What are you going to do?'

'Take twenty of your men with swords and bring Hercules to me,' said Zorin. 'We're going to kill him.'

Crisalt got twenty men together and went to get Hercules. 'Quickly!' he told them.

But they were too late. When they got to the tent, there was nobody there.

'He's not here!' cried Crisalt. 'How did he get away? We tied his arms and legs. But how –?' Then he knew. 'He's too strong to tie up! He can break anything! Now what do we do?'

♦

The men outside Zorin's tent saw somebody coming. 'Go away!' one of them cried.

Hercules walked on.

'Did you hear me?' called Zorin's man. 'Get away from here, or you're going to be dog food!'

Hercules pulled the two men to him, then threw them on the floor. He kicked another away from the door of the tent, and walked inside.

Zorin looked up from his chair. 'Hercules!' he cried.

'I want the Sword of Fire,' Hercules told him.

Zorin jumped up from his chair and ran behind it. 'You want the Sword of Fire?' he cried. 'You want the Fire?'

Hercules pulled the two men to him, then threw them on the floor.

23

Hercules saw a red light . . . and the light started to get bigger and bigger.

The Sword of Fire was beautiful. Zorin had it in front of him. 'Come and get it,' he said, and smiled. He moved the sword across the floor, and a line of fire followed it.

'Hephaestus wants it back,' said Hercules.

'He can't have it,' said Zorin.

'You're making a mistake, Zorin,' said Hercules.

'No, Hercules. *You* made the mistake,' said Zorin. 'You came into my tent, and now you're going to die.'

'Hephaestus is angry,' said Hercules. 'He wants −'

'Then he must come and get it,' said Zorin. He looked at the Sword of Fire, and smiled. 'This is a god's sword, and it's a god-killer.'

Hercules tried to think of a plan − quickly.

'Give me the Fire. I'll give it back to Hephaestus,' he said. 'Then you and I can talk about your Big Plan with King Arclin.'

Zorin laughed. 'So you know about that,' he said. 'Well, you aren't going to tell anybody.' He made a line of fire with the sword, and Hercules jumped back.

Suddenly Crisalt ran into the tent, followed by ten or twelve men.

'Hercules is −!' cried Crisalt. He saw Hercules and stopped.

Hercules pulled one of the raiders to him, and pushed him across the line of fire. Zorin put up his hand to stop the man, but the Sword of Fire hit the man. There was a sudden white light . . . then it was red again . . . and the man was not there!

Hercules didn't have time to think. He jumped at Zorin and pulled the Sword of Fire from his hands. He ran behind Zorin's chair and found the Sword's sheath. He quickly pushed the Sword into the sheath and ran out of the tent. Crisalt jumped at him, but Hercules kicked him to the floor and ran on.

Zorin's men came after him. He could hear them behind him but he ran on. He took the Sword of Fire out of its sheath and

Flames flew up into the sky.

ran to the nearest tent. There he used the sword to cut a line of fire across it. Flames flew up into the sky. He did the same to the next tent, and the next. More flames flew into the sky. He did not use the Sword of Fire on men. He was not Zorin. But tent after tent went up in flames and thick black smoke.

Zorin's men forgot about Hercules and started to run. Many of them ran out of the camp.

'Hercules!'

He turned and saw Crisalt running across to him. The man's face was black with smoke, and his arms were burned.

'Go away, Crisalt,' said Hercules.

'I-I'm going to kill you,' said Crisalt. But he was weak and tired after fighting the flames.

'Go home,' said Hercules. 'You're tired.'

'No,' said Crisalt.

'Then go to sleep,' said Hercules, and hit him hard on the head. Crisalt fell and did not move.

Chapter 9 Hercules' Next Fight

Soon Hercules was out of the camp.

'I did it,' he thought. 'I got the Sword of Fire. That's all I must do. But . . . there's Zorin.' He tried to think. 'I burned his tents, and most of his men ran away. It's time to go.'

He looked up and cried, 'Hermes! Come here! I know you can hear me.'

Hermes was suddenly in front of him.

Hercules gave him the Sword of Fire in its sheath. 'Take it to Hephaestus,' said Hercules. 'Take it, quickly.'

Hermes smiled. 'You did it! You burned half a mountain to get it, but Hephaestus is going to be very happy.'

They looked back and saw a man watching them from a

hundred metres away, with the burning camp behind him. Zorin.

'His fighting days are finished,' said Hermes.

'No, they're not,' said Hercules. 'He can find men to follow him again. And then there's Arclin. Can Arclin and Zorin work together now? Perhaps not. But Zorin can go to some other place and start again.'

'But he doesn't have the Sword of Fire,' said Hermes.

'No, he doesn't. Take it to Hephaestus,' said Hercules.

Hermes flew away with the Sword of Fire. Then Hercules walked back to Zorin. He stopped ten metres away from the raider.

'I'm going to get more men, and I'm going to come after you,' said Zorin. He had his sword in his hand.

The flames from the burning tents were hot on Hercules' face. He did not speak.

The flames from the burning tents were hot on Hercules' face.

Zorin smiled. 'Come and fight,' he said. He moved his sword left and right. 'Come on!'

'There are no men with you now,' said Hercules. 'When did *you* last fight somebody, Zorin? Don't you want any help?'

'No!' said Zorin.

And he ran at Hercules with an angry cry. Hercules turned away easily from Zorin's sword, and Zorin ran at him again. This time his sword cut into Hercules' arm. But he turned and hit Zorin across the back of the head, and the raider went down on to the grass.

He got up again. Slowly. Hercules waited.

Zorin ran at him again. This time Hercules got his arms round the raider and hit the sword out of his hand. They fell together on to the grass, and Zorin tried to get his teeth into Hercules' arm. Over and over they went on the grass.

Zorin was on his feet first. He tried to kick Hercules, but Hercules caught his foot. 'Sorry, Zorin,' Hercules said, and hit the raider on the head.

It was finished. Zorin's eyes turned up to the sky and closed, and he did not move. Hercules sat down on the grass. He was tired, too.

He watched two or three raiders walking away from the burning tents. They looked across at him, but did not stop.

'What am I going to do with Zorin?' he thought. 'I can't leave him here. And I can't kill him because I'm not a killer.'

Then he smiled. He had a plan.

He put Zorin on his back and started to walk away from the burning tents. Nobody stopped him. One raider with grey hair looked at Zorin when Hercules went past.

'Is he dead?' he asked Hercules.

'No,' said Hercules.

'Do you want me to kill him for you?' said the raider. 'I never liked him.'

Hercules smiled and said, 'No, thank you.'

Some hours later, Zorin made a sound and tried to move.

'Go back to sleep,' Hercules told him, and hit him again.

Chapter 10 King Arclin's New Plan

It was the afternoon, and Hercules could see King Arclin's city in front of him. Zorin saw the city and fought to get away.

'Don't,' said Hercules. 'I can easily put you to sleep again.'

'This is a mistake,' said Zorin.

Hercules laughed. 'I know your plan,' he said. 'And I know Arclin's plan. You and he want more and more towns and villages, and more and more money. Am I right?'

'I've got a lot of money,' said Zorin. 'Put me down, and you can have half of it.'

'Thank you, but no,' said Hercules. 'I've got all I want.'

'Listen, you don't know Arclin,' said Zorin. 'You want him to do something for you? Well, he's not going to do it. I know him.'

People started to follow them through the city to King Arclin's house.

'Kill him!' Zorin told the man outside the door.

The man looked at Hercules and at Zorin.

'Take me to King Arclin,' said Hercules.

'Don't do it!' cried Zorin.

Hercules hit him again, and Zorin's head fell again.

The captain was with King Arclin. Hercules heard Arclin say, 'Hercules did that! And you didn't kill him?' before he pushed open the door and walked into the room.

Arclin saw him. 'You!' he cried.

Hercules walked down the centre of the room to the two men. He threw Zorin down on the floor, next to the captain, then went to Arclin's chair. He put out one hand and pulled

Arclin up out of it. They were nose to nose.

'I know everything,' he said. 'I know about your plan, and I know Zorin's plan. You're working together, right? Or you were. Now I know the plan, too – so it isn't going to work. OK?'

'This is … I'm going to … my people …' King Arclin tried to find the right words, but couldn't.

'How old are you?' said Hercules. 'Twenty?'

'Y-yes,' said Arclin.

He looked at the captain. 'Captain, go and get something to tie up that man,' he said.

'And the people loved your father, is that right?' Hercules went on.

'Perhaps,' said the king. 'Yes, they did.'

'And you're angry because they don't love you as much as they loved him,' said Hercules.

'No … well … yes, perhaps.' King Arclin was unhappy. 'I try very hard,' he said. 'I want them to have more places to live, I want them to have more money. But all I hear is, "He's not as clever as his father." And I get angry!'

The captain came back with twelve men and they tied Zorin up.

Hercules did not look at them. 'OK,' he said to King Arclin. 'Listen, because I'm only going to say this once. Forget about trying to get your hands on everything in the world. And stop trying to be the same as your father. You're not him, you're you. Do the things that *you* think are best for your people.' He smiled. 'Your father was a good teacher, so you can do it.'

'Perhaps you're right,' Arclin said.

Hercules moved nearer and spoke quietly but coldly. 'Do it! And remember, I'm always nearer than you think.'

Arclin's face went white.

'Sir!' called the captain. 'What do you want me to do with Zorin?'

Hercules smiled back. 'You're going to be OK,' he said.

'Put him away,' Arclin said, when he could speak. 'And listen to me carefully. *He's not going to get away.* Do you understand? Forget the old days. Things are going to be different now. He must not get away.' He turned and smiled at Hercules.

Hercules smiled back. 'You're going to be OK,' he said.

Chapter 11 In the Village of Markan

That night, Hercules sat under the night sky and smiled happily. 'I've got nothing to do, nobody to help, nobody to fight,' he thought. 'That's good, because I want to stop for a week or two.'

'Hello,' said somebody above him.

Hercules didn't turn his head. 'Did you take the Sword of Fire back?' he asked. 'I hope he was happy.'

'He says, "Thank you." But he's going to find another summer home. That place was too noisy,' said Hermes.

Hercules shut his eyes.

'Are you all right?' asked Hermes. 'What's wrong with you? Look at those cuts on your arm! Why don't you −?'

'Hermes, go away,' said Hercules. 'Thank you for all your help, but go away.'

◆

Bestor saw him first. Then more and more people started to call, 'Thank you!' to him, and walk with him to the village square.

'Hercules,' said Bestor. 'You're back!' He ran across.

Hercules put a hand on the boy's arm and smiled at him. 'Thank you, Bestor,' he said. 'How's your father? Where is he?'

'Well . . .' Bestor began.

Hercules stopped smiling. 'Is he well? Did he get back OK?'

'Yes, he did,' said Bestor.

Hercules sat down and was happy.

Hercules sat down and was happy.

Then Hercules saw the flowers, and the long tables in the street. And the men and women wearing their best shirts and dresses.

'What's happening?' said Hercules. Then he saw Nikos and Lydia near the hotel. Nikos wore his best coat and trousers, and Lydia wore a pretty dress and had flowers in her hair.

'Are they husband and wife now?' asked Hercules.

'Yes, from today!' said Bestor.

♦

Later Hercules ate and drank with Nikos and Lydia, and with the happy people of the village. He answered all their questions. And when it was dark, and everything was quiet, Hercules left Markan and began walking east.

'What am I going to see tomorrow?' he thought. 'Who will I meet on the road? What will happen to me?' And then he laughed. '*Something* will – because I'm Hercules!'

1 Step completed on 20/04/2013

ACTIVITIES

Chapters 1–3

Before you read

1 Look quickly at the pictures in the book. What is the story about?
2 Find these words in your dictionary. The words are all in the story.
   *arrow   bone   bow   to burn   cart   flame   forest   god   grass
   raider   to steal   stick   sword   to tie*
   a Which words are in the picture?

   b What are the other words in your language?

After you read

3 Who are these people? What do we know about them?
   a Trax and Castus   **c** Hercules
   b Nikos, Bestor and Lydia   **d** Zorin
4 Who says these words? Who or what are they talking about?
   a 'He didn't give us our money.'
   b 'Bones – in the forest!'
   c 'Please stop that.'
   d 'We're going to burn that down.'
   e 'They're going back to Zorin . . .'

Chapters 4–7

Before you read

5 Why are Hercules and Nikos going to take the raiders to King Arclin? What do you think?

6 Find these words in your dictionary. Put them in the sentences.

captain   protect   tent

   a Please . . . . . me from the dangerous men!

   b The . . . . . and his men are fighters.

   c We slept in a . . . . . last night.

After you read

7 Answer these questions.

   a What is Zorin's plan for Hercules?

   b What is Hermes' job?

   c What does Hephaestus want? Who has it?

   d Why are Zorin and King Arclin working together?

   e Who kills Theo?

8 Work with a friend.

   Student A: You are Lydia. Nikos is in Markan again. Ask him questions about his time with Hercules.

   Student B: You are Nikos. Answer Lydia's questions.

Chapters 8–11

Before you read

9 Read this sentence from the story. Answer the questions. What do you think?

'Hercules gave him the Sword of Fire in its sheath.'

   a What do you put in a *sheath*?

   b How does Hercules get the Sword of Fire?

   c Who does he give it to?

After you read

10 Talk about King Arclin and his father. What is Arclin's problem? Do you know people with this problem?

11 How does the story finish for:

   a Hercules?   **c** Arclin?

   b Nikos?   **d** Zorin?

Writing

12 Write the story of the book in only five or six sentences.

13 You are King Arclin. Write a letter to Hercules. What did you do in the old days? How are you different now?

14 What did you like about the book? What did you not like? Write about it for your friends.

15 Write a different Hercules story. Who is in the story? What happens? How does the story end?